ANIMAL COLORING BOOK

This Book Belongs To

....

....

....

COLOR TEST PAGE

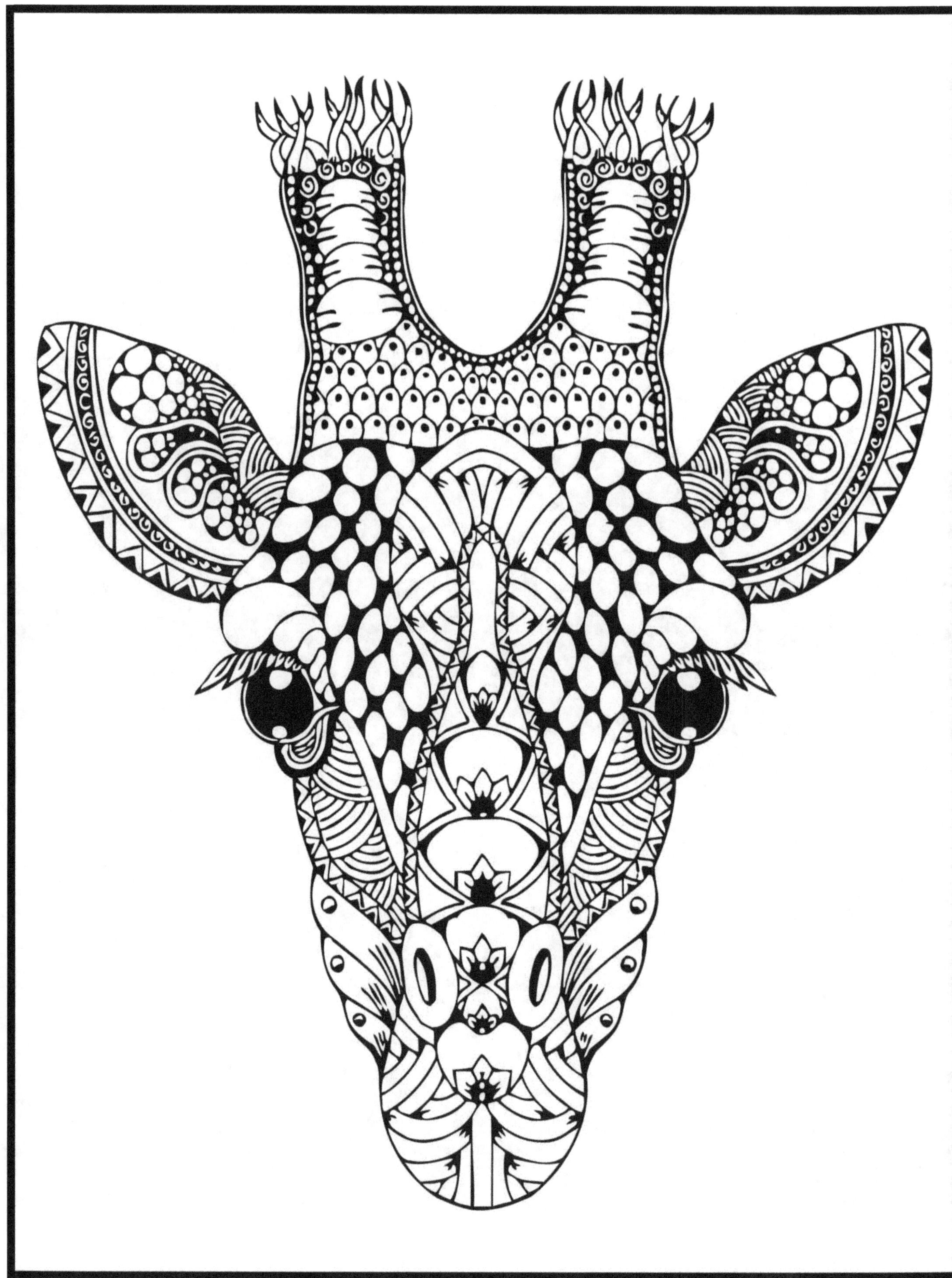

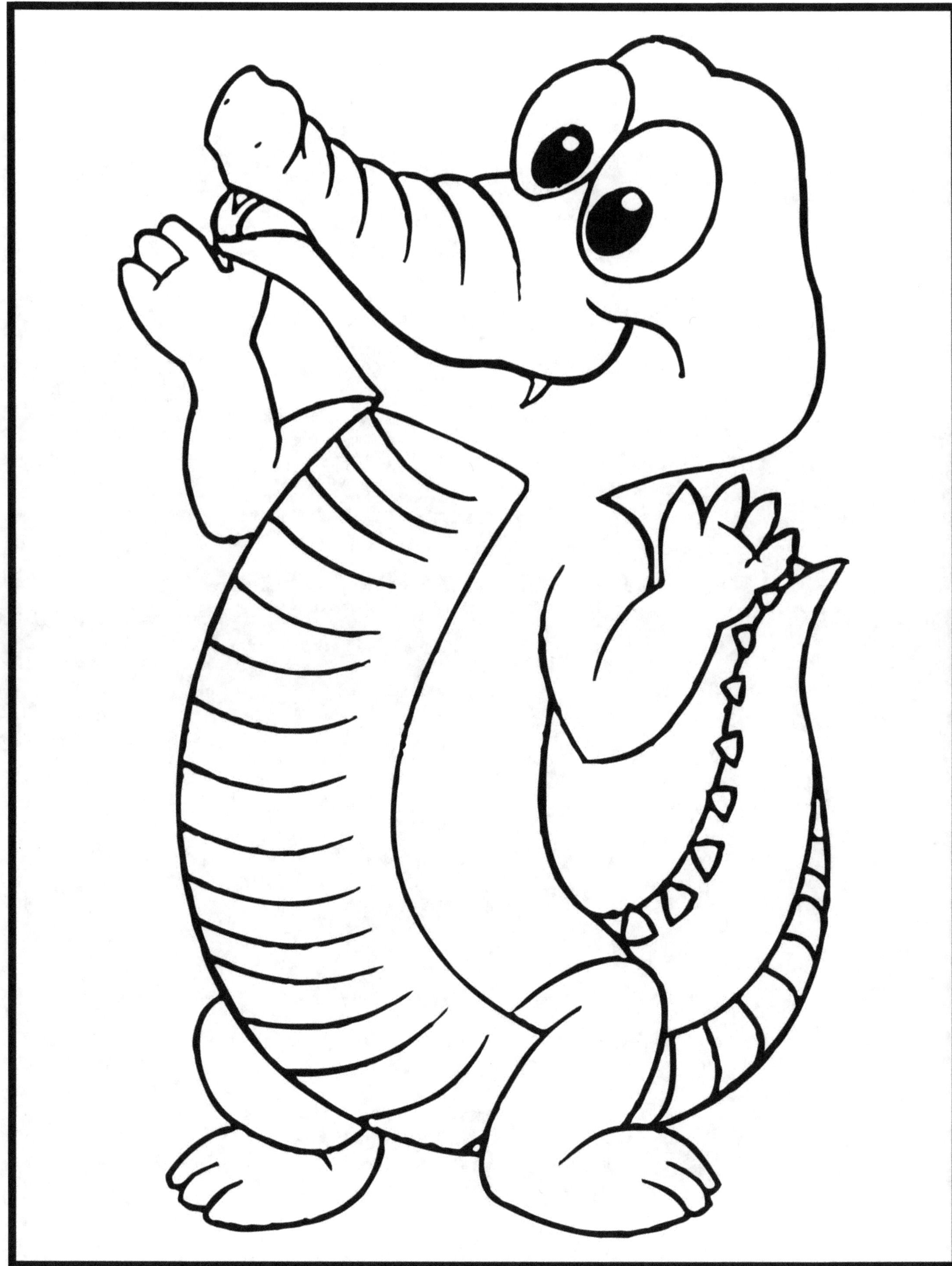

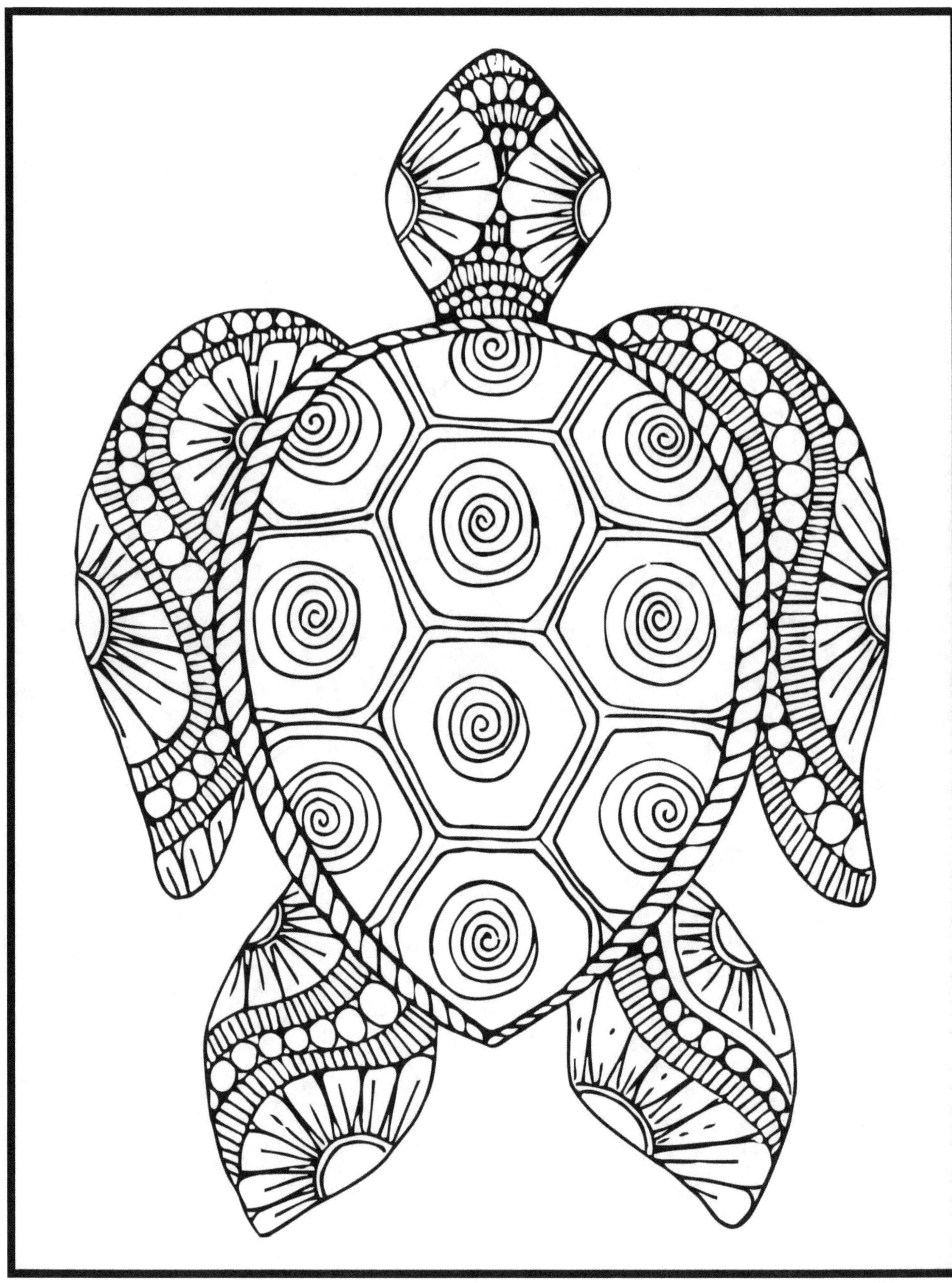

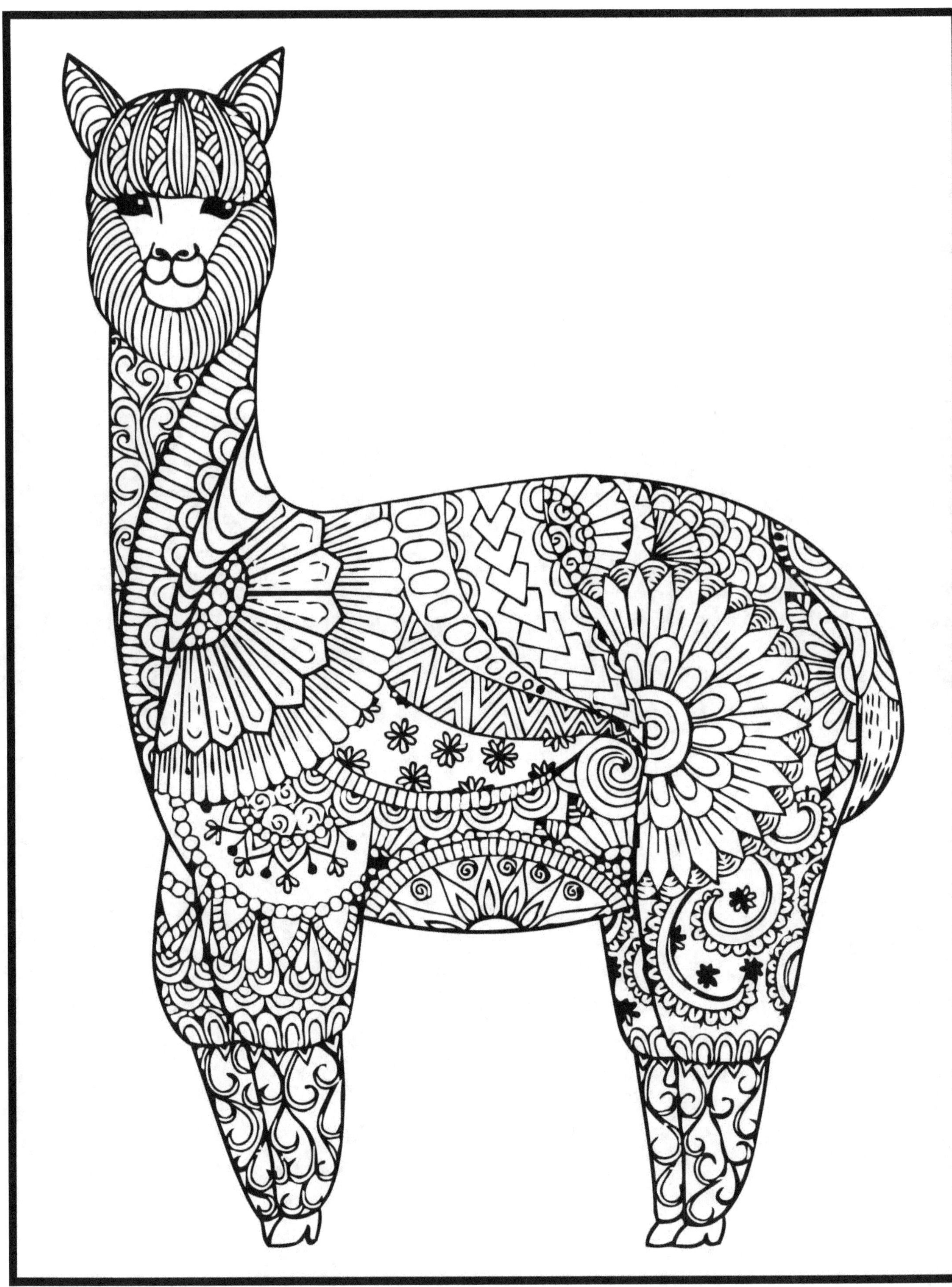

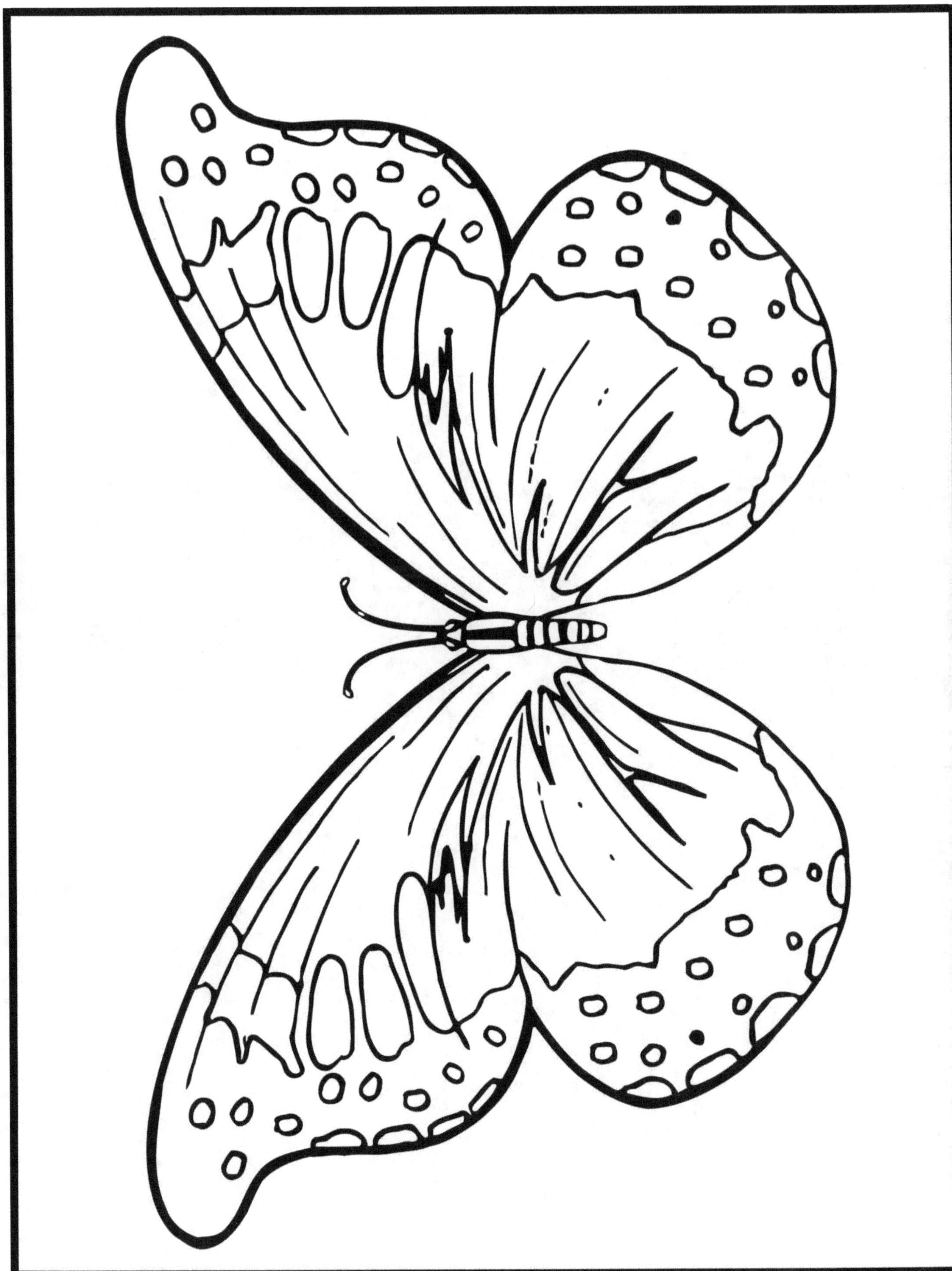

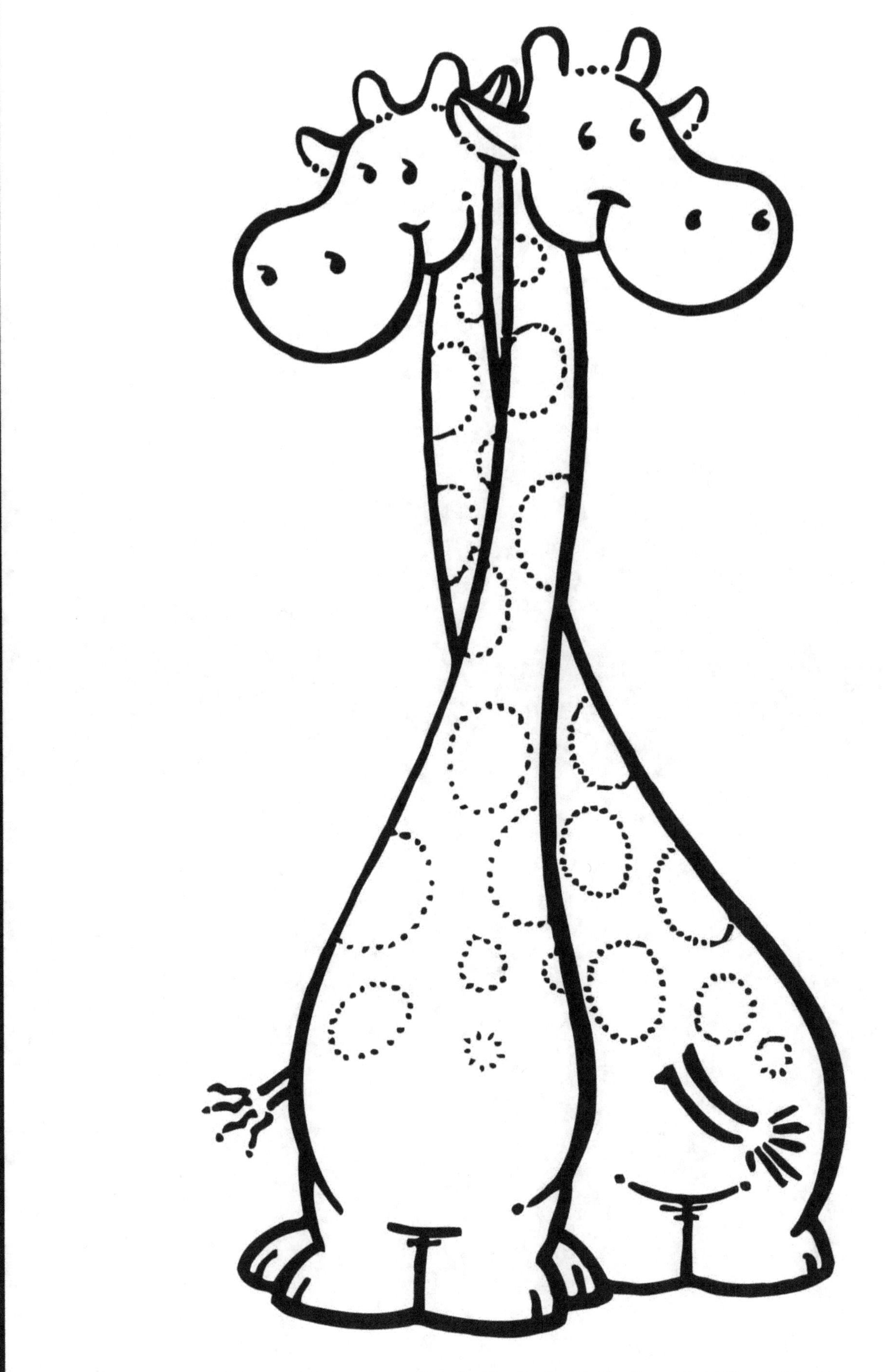

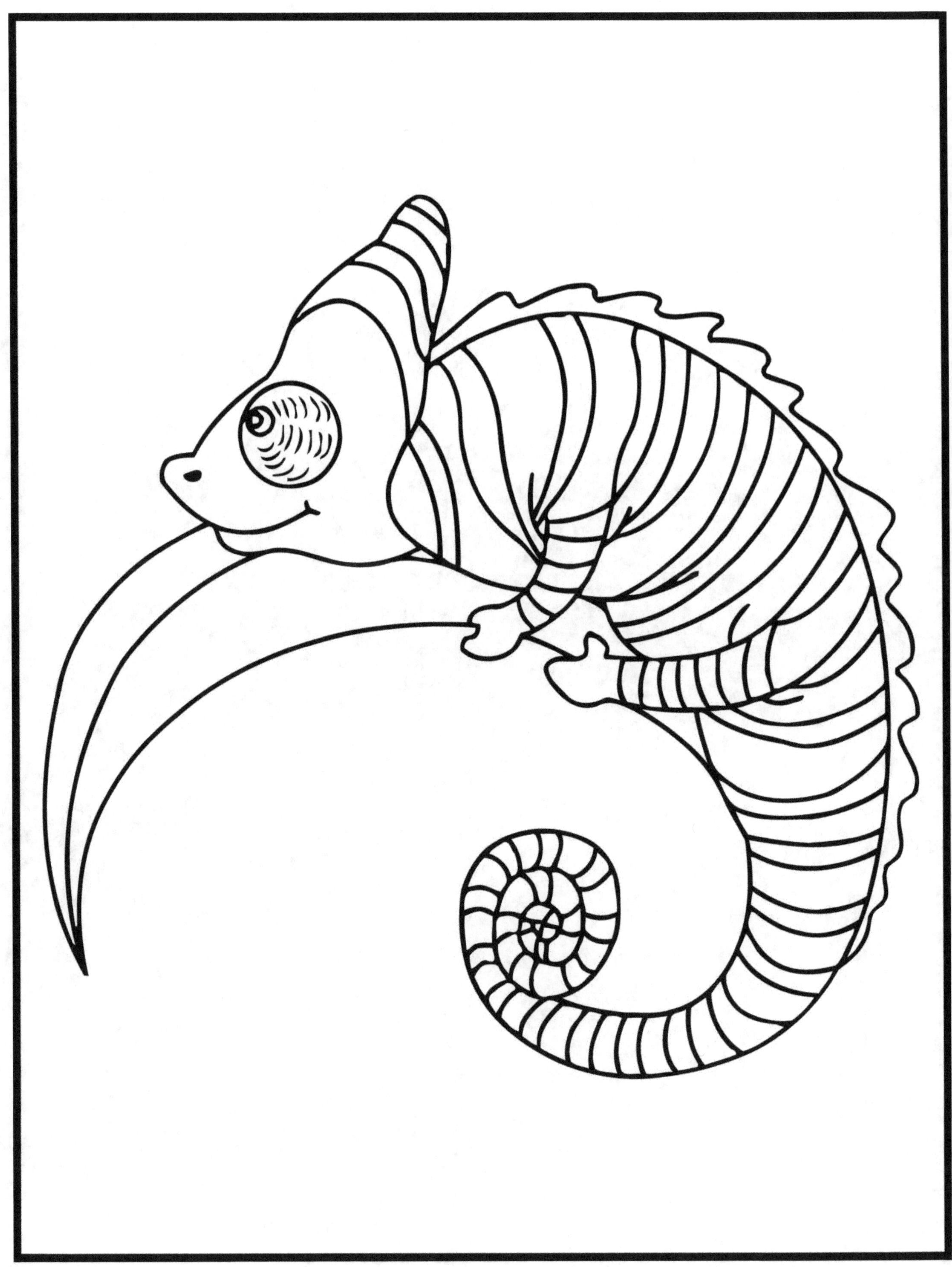

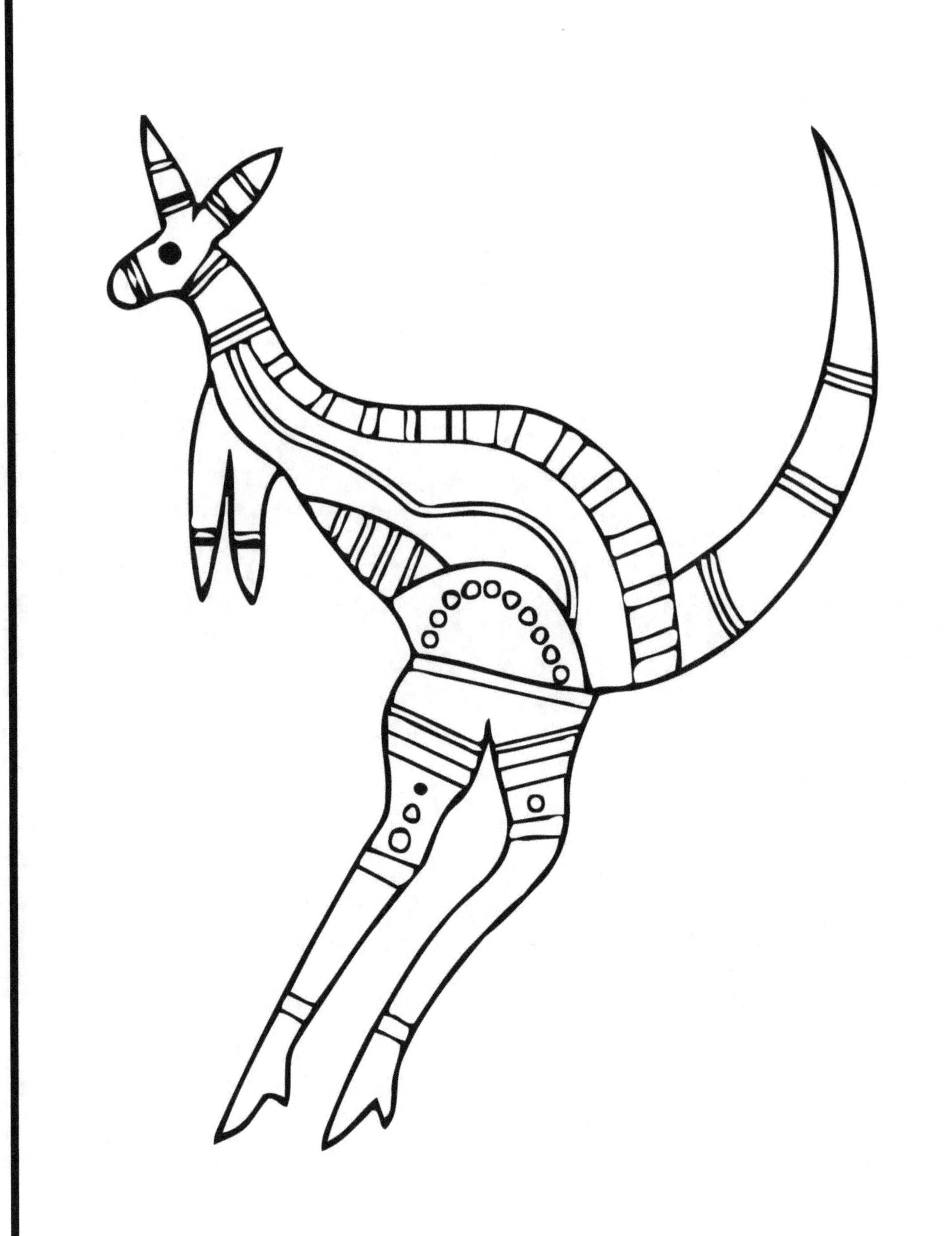